A New True Book

MOUNTAIN LIONS

By David Petersen

CHILDRENS PRESS ®

CHICAGO

A mountain lion
sharpens its claws.

PHOTO CREDITS

H. Armstrong Roberts–© E. Degginger, 17

Root Resources–© Mary & Lloyd McCarthy,
Cover, 24; © Byron Crader, 4; © Kenneth W.
Fink, 11; © Diana Stratton, 33

Tom Stack & Associates–© Thomas Kitchin, 7
(bottom), 41; © Robert Winslow, 26, 36

SuperStock International, Inc.–© D. Northcott,
8

Tony Stone Images–© Tom Tietz, 44

Unicorn Stock Photos–© Fred Reischl, 21;
© Robert W. Ginn, 32

Valan–© S. J. Krasemann, 2, 20, 42, 43;
© Dennis Schmidt, 7 (top), 29; © Esther
Schmidt, 30; © James D. Markou, 40, 45

Visuals Unlimited–© Leonard Rue III, 13;
© Tom J. Ulrich, 14; © Joe McDonald, 18, 22,
35, 37; © Charles Heidecker, 23; © Don W.
Fawcett, 27; © Ron Spomer, 38

COVER: Mountain lion and cub

Project Editor: Fran Dyra
Design: Margrit Fiddle
Photo Research: Feldman & Associates, Inc.

Library of Congress Cataloging-in-Publication Data

Petersen, David.
    Mountain lions / by David Petersen.
        p.   cm.–(A New true book)
    Includes index.

    ISBN 0-516-01077-8
    1.   Pumas–Juvenile literature.   [1.   Pumas.]
I.   Title.
QL737.C23P425 1995
599.74'428–dc20
94-36353
CIP
AC

TABLE OF CONTENTS

A deer pauses to drink at the water's edge.

A DEADLY HUNTER

Imagine a deer standing near a quiet lake in the Rocky Mountains. With its big eyes, it searches the area for enemies. Its nose tests the breeze for any scent of danger. Its huge ears turn this way and that—listening, listening.

Finally the deer is satisfied that it is alone and safe. It walks to the water's edge.

But the deer has been fooled. It is not alone, and it is far from safe. A deadly hunter lurks nearby.

On big, quiet paws, the hunter creeps toward the deer. Its earth-colored fur blends in with its surroundings, making it almost invisible. The hunter's scent is blown away from the deer by the wind.

The hunter is a mountain lion—almost close enough to strike. Tensing its

shoulder muscles
and extending its
claws, the lion waits.
When the deer puts
its head down to

The mountain lion is a
swift and deadly hunter.
Deer (right) are the
mountain lion's main prey.

drink, the mountain lion
springs forward in a
lightning-fast leap.
But the deer is even

A lion leaps forward to pounce on a prey animal.

faster. In the split second the lion is in the air, the deer senses danger and takes flight.

The chase is on. For a moment it seems the lion will catch its prey. But—just in time—the deer breaks out of the forest. In the open meadow, it can run at full speed.

Immediately, the mountain lion realizes it has lost the race. Panting for breath, it gives up.

Mountain lions have small lungs. They become "winded" after only a brief, fast chase. A healthy deer can run for miles, so the lion must catch the deer quickly or it will not catch it at all.

This deer was healthy. If it had been very old, or very young, or ill, the lion would have caught it. If the deer's vision, hearing, and sense of smell had not been perfect, it would not have escaped.

Lions move slowly and quietly to get near their prey.

PREDATORS

Mountain lions are predators—animals that catch other animals for food. Predators hunt weak, sick, or slow animals because they are easier to

11

catch. By killing these weaker animals, they help keep the species they hunt for food healthy.

Predators also help keep populations of deer and other animals from growing too large.

In some areas, lions and other predators have been removed from the ecosystem. Then the populations of herbivorous, or plant-eating, animals

Mountain lion chasing a snowshoe hare

such as deer and rabbits
have grown so large that
they eat all the available
food. When winter comes,
many animals starve.
Predators help prevent
such disasters.

THE AMERICAN LION

The mountain lion is known by more than one hundred names! Its best-known names are cougar, puma, and panther. Before Europeans arrived, the mountain lion was the most widespread large mammal in the Americas. It roamed from the Atlantic Ocean to the Pacific Ocean, and from South America north through Canada.

Over the years, humans have taken over the mountain lion's hunting lands. Thousands of lions have been killed by hunters. In the United States today, the big cat survives in healthy numbers only in the western states and in southern Texas.

Smaller lion populations are found in parts of Louisiana and Arkansas. And miraculously, a tiny population still survives in

Mountain lions are still found in southern Texas. This one seems to be sharpening its claws on a giant cactus.

the East and in southwest Florida. But there are no mountain lions at all left in the Midwest.

THE FLORIDA PANTHER

   The Florida mountain lion is called the Florida panther. It is separated from its western cousins by 2,000 miles (3219 kilometers) or more.

   The Florida panther is the rarest type of mountain lion. It is also the rarest large mammal in North America.

Opposite page: The Florida panther is endangered.

Miami Beach, Florida. The building of cities and
towns has reduced the panther's habitat.

Homes and shopping centers are spreading all over
Florida, covering islands and coastal areas.

As Florida has become
more crowded with people,
most of the panther's
hunting ground has been
taken over for homes,
highways, and shopping
centers.

Without enough land on
which to hunt and hide

21

The Florida panther needs wild areas to live in.

from danger, the panther cannot survive. Today, only 30 to 50 adult panthers remain in the wild, barely holding on.

But the Florida panther is not yet lost. Many

people are working to see that it does not disappear entirely. If its remaining habitat can be saved, perhaps this beautiful and rare creature will not have to follow the dinosaurs into extinction.

Hopefully, this Florida panther cub will not be one of the last of its kind.

CAT OF ONE COLOR

The mountain lion's scientific name is *Felis concolor*, which is Latin for "cat of one color." But that name is misleading. Although most of its fur is a yellowish or tan color, its belly and parts of its face are white.

The mountain lion has patches of black and white fur on its face.

It also has black markings on its face and a black tip at the end of its long tail. Its eyes are the color of amber.

Mountain lions snarl, scream, purr, and hiss. They also have a soft whistle call. But unlike African lions, they do not roar.

An angry mountain lion may hiss and snarl like a house cat.

Nor are they as large as their African relatives. The average adult male mountain lion weighs from 125 to 175 pounds (57 to 79 kilograms). A full-grown male may be 9 feet (2.7 meters) long, including a tail that measures 2 to 3 feet (61 to 91 centimeters). Females are smaller.

Biologists believe the mountain lion uses its long tail for balance when leaping after prey, jumping

The mountain lion's long tail may help it keep
its balance when running or jumping.

down from trees or rocks,
or bounding from boulder
to boulder.

These powerful cats can
jump as far as 30 feet (9
meters) and as high as 15
feet (4.6 meters).

EARNING
A LION'S LIVING

Deer are the mountain lion's favorite food, but it also hunts elk, raccoons, birds, and many other animals. Sometimes it even catches porcupines and skunks.

Unlike wolves and coyotes, mountain lions are lone stalkers. They do not hunt in groups.

Opposite page: A mountain lion perches in a tree. High above the ground, the lion can see prey animals a long way off.

If you've ever watched a house cat sneaking up on a bird, you know exactly how a mountain lion hunts. Using trees, rocks, brush, and tall grass to hide its approach, the big

Members of the cat family may be large or small, but they all hunt in much the same way.

A male mountain lion stalking its prey

cat crouches close to the
ground. It creeps
forward—one careful step
at a time. When it is only
a few feet from its prey, it
pounces.

When a mountain lion catches its prey, it uses its sharp canine teeth to bite the victim behind the head and kill it quickly.

Once a mountain lion has made a kill, it drags its meal to a sheltered place to eat. An adult lion can eat as much as 10 pounds (4.5 kilograms) of

A mountain lion feeds on a deer it killed.

meat at one time. That's
the same as 20 big
hamburgers!

When it has eaten its
fill, the lion covers the
remains of its kill with
leaves, dirt, or snow. It

then moves off a short
distance to nap and guard
its food. Every now and then,
it returns to eat some more.

A mountain lion naps on a rock ledge.

The mountain lion kills its prey quickly with a bite to the neck.

Mountain lions and other meat eaters do not kill for fun. They hunt because they are hungry. They must catch enough food to feed themselves and their young, or starve to death.

Male and female mountain lions. People rarely
see these shy animals in the wild.

RAISING A FAMILY

Most of the year,
mountain lions live alone.
But when a female is
ready to raise a family,
she spends a couple of
weeks with a male in
order to mate.

If the mating is successful,
the female moves to a
small cave or rocky crevice.
Three months later, one to
six cubs are born.

At birth, the cubs weigh

less than 1 pound (0.5 kilogram). Their fur is spotted, their tails have dark rings, and their eyes are shut.

The newborn cubs begin nursing immediately, and grow quickly. Within two

Mountain lion mother and cubs

A mountain lion cub. The spotted fur helps it hide from enemies.

weeks, their eyes are open. In about a month, they start eating meat brought to them by their mother.

At about two months of age, the cubs start following

Mother mountain lion teaching her cubs how to hunt

their mother on her hunts.
Play is an important part
of learning to hunt. The
frisky cubs stalk, wrestle,
bite, and pounce on one

another. They are strengthening muscles and developing the skills they need to become successful hunters.

Cubs wrestle each other and tumble about. They are learning the skills they will need for hunting.

This older mountain lion cub will soon be ready to leave its mother.

After 18 to 24 months,
the young lions are able
to find their own food.
Then they leave home to
hunt and live alone.

Most people will never see a mountain lion in the wild. But isn't it thrilling to know that such big, beautiful, mysterious creatures still roam free in North America today?

WORDS YOU SHOULD KNOW

biologist (by • AHL • uh • jist)–a scientist who studies living things

canine teeth (KAY • nine TEETH)–long, sharp teeth in the front of the mouth

crevice (KREH • viss)–a narrow opening, such as a crack in a rock

ecosystem (EE • koh • siss • tim)–a community of living things that function together as a unit and depend on one another

extinction (ex • TINK • shun)–the complete dying out of a species of plant or animal

Felis concolor (FEE • liss KAHN • ko • ler)–the scientific name for the mountain lion

habitat (HAB • ih • tat)–home; a place where an animal can find everything it needs to live

herbivorous (her • BIV • er • uss)–plant-eating; living on plants rather than meat

invisible (in • VIZ • ih • bil)–not visible; cannot be seen

meadow (MEH • doh)–a grassy area with few trees

misleading (mis • LEE • ding)–causing someone to believe what is not true or not completely true

population (pah • pyoo • LAY • shun)–the total number of animals of the same kind living in the same place at the same time

predator (PREH • duh • ter)–an animal that kills and eats other animals

prey (PRAY)–animals that are hunted for food by predators

scent (SENT)—odor; smell

scientific name (sye • in • TIH • fik NAIM)–a name, usually from the Latin language, given by scientists to a plant or animal species

species (SPEE • sheez)–a particular type of plant or animal that is distinct from all others

stalk (STAWK)—to creep up on something, such as a prey animal, without being seen

surroundings (sir • ROUN • dingz)–the conditions or things around an animal or a place

survive (sir • VYVE)–to last; to remain alive after great danger or trouble

INDEX

About the Author

David Petersen lives in a cabin in mountain lion country in Colorado. He has studied mountain lions, and he participated in the Colorado Division of Wildlife's 1991 Mountain Lion-Human Interaction Symposium and Workshop.